What I Would Have Told You

A Collection of Poetry

Lauren Monica

Vienna Publishing

ISBN: 979-8-9887867-0-2

*dedicated to those who broke my heart
and to those who made it whole again*

CONTENTS

Bloom

A Watercolor Love

our love is a watercolor painting
i'm purple and you're blue
i can't see which part is only me
and which part is only you

we drift together until we've
faded into a color all our own
we're better now that we're together
than we ever were alone

The Melody of Your Mind

you invited me to dance with you
in the depths of your mind

Evolution

embrace me as if
i were your own
a musing of your thought
a reflection of your desire
hold me as if
i belong to you
like you need another hit
and i'm your supplier

speak to me as if
you already know
i'll understand
just voicing your thoughts
to hear the words
leave my lips
and fall where you
knew they would land

we become a united reflection
in a mirror that works both ways
taking two opposing images
and putting their entangled
result on display

not knowing what comes next
but knowing what's present now
we take from each other what's given
because now we know
what we're allowed

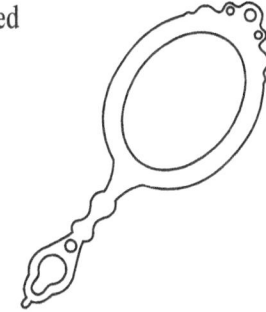

Lauren Monica

Through My Eyes

what you saw as flaws
i saw as perfection
if only you could see yourself
through my eyes

The Ease of Us

you felt like a sunday morning
i wanted to live in those moments

Below the Surface

your rough hands
soothe my gentle spirit
making me feel
raw and open
ready to accept
all you have to give

pull me into a world
i never knew was there
a part for me that
has always been waiting
just below the surface

it's safe now that
my hand is in yours
as you guide me
giving me your eyes to see

the world looks so different
through your rose-colored view
what was bleak has turned bright
an invitation into the living

the fear is slowly settling now
as i can fully exhale
i feel the world hold me up
and give me strength
through its sudden
all-consuming presence

i'm supported by the truth
that's always been there
only ever just a little ways
below the surface

Reflection

your eyes moved over me
like i was a blank canvas
for you to add to
you painted me
in the image you saw
a reflection of your love
i never knew i could be so
beautiful

A Piece of Me

i sacrificed a piece of me
so you could be whole
that little piece of me
fit perfectly in that
missing piece of you

The Words A Kiss Hold

i tasted the words
"i love you"
as they fell from your lips
to mine

Bloom

i bloomed
for the first time
while being held
in your arms

Meant Only for Me

speak to me in code
the one only i understand
the phrases and words
buried under the palms
of your hands

the stories your lips tell
meant only for me
the parts of your world
that just i'm meant to see

What I Would Have Told You

you string them together
into an epic tale of desire
each line that i learn
i'm brought higher and higher

into this melodrama
written just for two
i know i'll love the ending
if the ending comes from you

When I'm With You

dance with me
whisper it'll
be alright
take my hand
and lead me into
the light

Bliss

those little things
don't seem to matter
when i'm yours
and you're mine

Synonymous

when i think of love
i think of you
of your poetic words
lingering touch
and welcome kiss
i guess in my mind
you and love will always be
synonymous

Radiant

i see you as you wish
you saw yourself
always under the glow
of a golden light

Carried in My Heart

i paint a picture of you
on the walls of my heart
so you'll always be with me
even when we're apart

The Sweetest Taste

when words fail
i'm left with only
your name on my lips

Lauren Monica

A Map to Us

i study you like a map
the freckle right above your lip
the way your front teeth gap
how your eyes change color
depending on the light
how you get a dimple when you smile
on your left side but not your right
how when you say "i love you"
it sounds like a kiss
how you watch me
when i walk into a room
leaving not one part unmissed
i study you like a map
and the best thing that i see
is that in the end it always
leads back to you and me

The Art of Love

your fingertips move over me
dancing softly to the beat of my heart
playing me like your favorite melody
turning our love into art

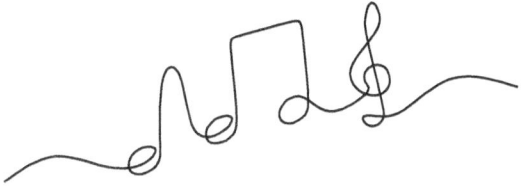

More Than Words

who was i without you
who was i before you
the way i love you
the way i see you
the way i feel you
is more than i can say
with words

A Physical Constellation

your lips told stories
on my body
that you never said
with words

A Momentary Regret

go slowly and take it all in
for soon it may just be
a memory

A Lover's Gamble

is it worth a broken heart
to say that you have loved

Purple

Lauren Monica

The Mirage

in the beginning
you tasted so sweet
i couldn't get enough
i wanted to drown in you
but with each day
you started to drift away
until one day our love
was only a mirage

A Ghost of Myself

each time i speak
my voice gets softer
quieted by your
indifference

Lauren Monica

An Absent Longing

i simply longed
for you to give
without me asking

Torn Between You

your words are like petals
your actions like thorns
is it worth it to love a rose
if your heart is always torn

Lauren Monica

At Your Hands

it's like you used to
leave on purpose
so i'd know what it was like
to starve in your absence
so i'd know how easily
you could take it all away

Broken Pieces

i collect broken things
broken promises
hoping to make them
whole again
trying desperately to take
what i've been given
and turn it into
what i deserve

Lauren Monica

The Fatal Equation

am i not supposed
to feel pain
is love pain
but pain is not love
your tone is stinging
your words slap me
where it hurts
am i wrong to
still love you
is pain not love

A Loud Silence

you listened
but never truly
heard me

How

how can i still love you
when i don't even like you
anymore

A Noose of Roses

maybe i loved the pain
the constant ups and downs
at least i knew i could feel

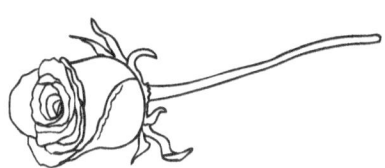

Blue

you gave me purple
when i asked for blue
knowing fully what i needed
but you only cared about you

Holding Onto Air

i was always on edge
waiting for you to tell me
we were done
i took all the pieces
you'd give me
until finally there
were none

Depleted Devotion

i wasn't your right
but a privilege
just because i was yours
at the start
does not mean that
i always will be

i am not an ever-flowing well
for you to draw from
if you do not nourish me
how do you expect me to
stay whole

how can i give
when there is
nothing to sustain
my soul
my body
my mind

What I Would Have Told You

you test me
you challenge me
you deplete me
until there is nothing left
this is when
you leave

I am hollow
unfilled by your devotion
you took all I had
leaving me with nothing

who am i if not
yours to draw from
i've forgotten who i am
for myself
i only know me
as you
for you
with you

Bitter
Fruit

Lauren Monica

The Noise in Silence

i'm looking through glass
trying to find how this ended
my reflection looks like you
and all the ways i've been upended

my mind feels forever shattered
like it will always be in pieces
there's so much noise I don't remember
as the silence around me increases

it's getting louder and louder
as i realize what you've said
"i don't love you anymore"
is all that's running through my head

Breathless

i'm not being poetic
my heart broke
when you left
the wind was knocked
from my lungs
my body literally
ached for you

Lauren Monica

An Unrecognizable Difference

did you ever love me
or did you just love
the love i gave you

No Longer

i gave up myself for us
but that meant
when there was
no longer an us
i could no longer
find me

Today

today I felt invisible
the days are catching up to me
today I felt alone
something all too familiar
today I cried
it was short but not sweet
today I missed you again
so I know I'm feeling weak

Wondering

i wonder if you
looked at the phone
as many times as i did
wondering if i'd call

Lauren Monica

The Distasteful Disposition

how do i make it stop
without letting it all go

The Declaration

i'm choking
all the air has been used up
there's no room for me in my stories
here and now is just a figment
and you can't hold on to that

Lost

when i'm lost
in crowded places
all i see is your face

Fiction

i wish our love story
was as great as people
thought it was

The Weight of Nothing

anytime something
new happened
i had to stop myself
from dialing your number
you weren't my person anymore
the emptiness was crushing

Dirty

your words still play
through my mind
like a symphony of pain
i try to understand
how such cruel words
could come from a mouth
that tasted so sweet
i wish i could wash them away
scrub every crevice of my mind
i thought they'd fade
but the stain has lasted with time

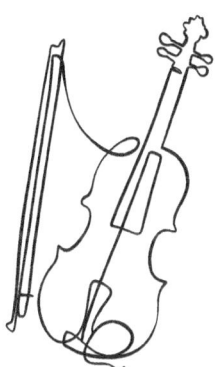

Different

i wish things had been different
that the sun had never set

Bitter Fruit

you stained me
with bitterness
so no one could have me
as sweet as you did

Tangled
in Feeling

Something

i want to feel something
well actually
i feel a lot of things
what i really mean is
i want to feel something
like i felt with you

The Ghost of You

the ghost of our love
still lingers long after
our last goodbye
appearing to remind me
of what was left behind

i see it in their
shallow eyes
in the conversation
that always seems too light
in the way he kisses me
that never feels quite right

how will i ever move on
with someone new
when all i can remember
is the ghost of you

Lauren Monica

Love as a Disguise

i'm trying not
to be the girl
i was with you
seeking anything but you
but us

let me reinvent myself
as someone who seeks
stable and secure

i think i've mistaken
passion for love
a lover for a partner
words for a promise

you showed me what
can hide beneath
the butterflies in my stomach
the lust that hangs over you
and the deceit of desire

it was never what it seemed
just love as a disguise
for a liar

Shallow

maybe if i just don't
fall that hard
this time
it won't be so difficult
to pick myself back up
again

Protecting Myself

i want to be numb
to wear my pain as armor
and to never again
be in so deep
because now i know what
it feels like to drown

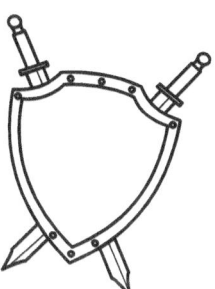

A Love Like Ours

i'm scared i'll never find
a love like ours again
what if you were
my once in a lifetime
and we were never
meant to end

The Shrinking Room

even after all you put me through
if i saw you again i don't know if
i'd be able to control myself
would passion beat out logic
would i let you destroy me
all over again

The Half the Time Truth

i miss you

My Heart Never Learns

my heart splits back open
each time i hear your name
remembering how you
used to be the one
who took away the pain

now i'm drowning
in our memories
in the way you
looked at me just right
how you used to send me
your beautiful words
each morning
and every night

i basked in the sweetness
the soft moments
your desperate touch
but i knew it then
just like i know it now
we were always just a little
too much

i guess it was toxic
if you look at it that way
but it didn't feel like
a mistake
all those years ago
or to this day

What I Would Have Told You

it just felt electric
like something
i never knew could exist
like you'd be mine forever
instead of now just when
i reminisce

i'm trying to learn
from those mistakes
find something
less all-consuming
a love that's
kind to my heart
but if i'm being honest
i don't even know
where to start

Lauren Monica

when i look at them
it's hard not to see you
all of the hurt from
when you left
but also all of the love
the moments shared
the understanding
the depth

my mind is
telling me one thing
trying to protect
my fragile heart
to look for
something easy
so my world doesn't
again fall apart

but when i look for easy
or even think i've
found it this time
my soul is never set on fire
like it was
when you were mine

my heart wants it
all-consuming
it wants the fire
even if it burns
my mind tries to
talk me out of it but
my heart just never learns

Senses

when the night is starry
i think of you
i remember how you told me once
when we were still in love
how even when we're apart
we can still see the same stars

when i hear that song
i think of you
how i always used to cry
when i heard it
i wonder if i still would

when he kisses me
i think of you
but the memory of
your touch is fading

i think about you all the time
i wonder if you ever think about me

Lauren Monica

Can't Catch a Feeling

each time I try
to replace you
i get more
disappointed

Fleeting

they ask me about the future
and i tell them about the past
trying to explain how
i've been conditioned
to believe that nothing
will ever last

Learning to Unlove

i didn't have to try
to love you
it was the easiest thing
i've ever done
what was hard
was learning how to
stop loving you
going from all of you
to none

My Favorite Day

today used to be
my favorite day
but now it just
passes by
i thought about
texting you
happy birthday
but was too afraid
you wouldn't reply

Lauren Monica

More Than Myself

you were my first
like seeing light
for the first time
you gave me gifts
i've never been given
and told me things
i've never before heard
i held onto our time
like the sky holds the sun

i feared the future
that one day this would
come to an end
how could i go on
without the air you gave me to breathe
how could i go on
without the eyes you gave me to see
how could i go on
when i loved you more than myself

What I Would Have Told You

you were my first
everything felt so strong
the hate and the love
we were like a mountain
in a field of grass
bigger was better
but also so much worse
because when it came falling down
it made the loudest sound

when a mountain falls
with no one but us around
how could anyone but you
know my hurt
then you ran from the scene
for it was you who made it fall

Lauren Monica

i was left melted into the earth
with nothing but my form
i laid there lifeless in thought
my deepest fear had come true
but i didn't fully know it yet
for when you left
you took my mind too

you took parts of me
without my say
i still don't know
if i'll ever get them back
but now years have gone by
and i've finally
gotten back my time

What I Would Have Told You

i say i've moved on
but you'll never fully leave
you've been planted in my heart
like the roots of a tree

when you are the first
it isn't the same
because you showed me
something i never knew
and sometimes fear
i'll never know again

how are you now
sitting on a distant dusty shelf
when years ago i loved you
more than myself

Lauren Monica

C'est La Vie

i think of you on my saddest days
the way you gave me a place to stay
a place of comfort
a hand to hold
the memories i lived
are now just stories told

all i can remember
is clouded by your touch
it used to make me smile
but now it's far too much

it was magnetic
even electric
an instantaneous spark
i try to get you out of my mind
but you left a lasting mark

i think of you on my saddest days
when i need a place to go
it's hard to break a habit
when it's all you used to know

but stories are rewritten
and endings sometimes change
life is full of puzzle pieces
for us to rearrange

so if it doesn't turn out
how you expected it to be
remember life goes on
remember c'est la vie

Lauren Monica

Revolving Around You

i'm stuck in a revolving door
that plays the memories of our past
sometimes it moves slowly
and sometimes it moves fast

there are memories i like to watch
and some i don't want to see
but i always slow down at the parts
when you were in love with me

An Innocent Love

i've decided to remember
us as we were that day
the innocent feeling
of young love
why tarnish something beautiful
with the mistakes of
what once was

Lauren Monica

Memories

i heard we're made up of memories
and if that happens to be true
it's a blessing and a curse
because that means i'm made up
of you

my mind is stained the
color of your eyes
your words play on repeat
i compare the memory
i've saved of you
to every person i meet

sometimes i take comfort
in the fact that you
live up in my head
but other times i wish
i could just turn it off
and exist in the present instead

i'm trying to start again
but you won't give me the space
my mind is cluttered with
moments and feelings
i fear i'll never replace

your spirit lives within me
because it's all i've ever known
i'm too afraid to forget
the memory of you
and risk being
all alone

Lauren Monica

The Ruins of Our Love

strawberry memories
stain the story i've saved
about you and me
a sweet red bleeds
all over the blank canvas
that i'd still never wish
was wiped clean

it may be a little messy
maybe a little less than ideal
but i'd gladly give you
my heart again
even knowing that pain
would be part of the deal

the stories are made of
smudged ink now
as time has slowly moved on
but the impact you made
and the home you
built within me
will never truly be gone

the foundation has surely shattered
the walls have long ago caved in
but the ruins of what was
still holds a place in my heart
always a reminder of what has
and could have been

Holding On

all i want to do
is make poetry
out of you
because at least then
you're still with me
even if only through
the words of my pen

A Transient Well

i'll write for you my
words of desperation
and i'll only let myself
cry until the ink has
run dry

A Desired Mistake

i would go through it all over again
even knowing our love
would eventually come to an end

Free

if the words won't come
does that finally mean
you don't own my heart anymore

Lauren Monica

What I Would Have Told You

what i would have told you
if i knew that was the last time
our final moment together
when i got to call you mine

i'd say i wish it had been easier
that we didn't drift apart
i'd ask you to hold on to the good times
and the piece i gave you of my heart

i'd hum the melody of our song
hoping it would get stuck in your head
afraid that one day you'd forget me
and all the things we left unsaid

What I Would Have Told You

i'd ask you to kiss me once more
before we made ourselves go
so i could remember
the way our lips danced
never too fast
and never too slow

the last thing i'd tell you
i'm sure you already knew
i'd send you off with that
piece of my heart
and the words
"i'll always love you"

ABOUT THE AUTHOR

Lauren Monica grew up outside of Boston and now lives in Austin (the poet in her only likes to live in places that rhyme). She studied Psychology and Sociology at the University of Texas at Austin. Hook 'em! She currently works as a social media manager, but her dream is to be a full-time poet and author. When not writing, she spends her time cuddled up on the couch with her two kitties and a good book, or with family. This is her debut poetry collection.

Connect with Lauren on Instagram: @laurenmonicawrites